Ludvigsen Library Series

CORVAIR by CHEVROLET

Experimental & Production Cars
1957 THROUGH 1969

Introduction by
Edward N. Cole

Iconografix

Iconografix
PO Box 446
Hudson, Wisconsin 54016 USA

Library of Congress Card Number: 2001131357

ISBN 1-58388-058-5

04 05 06 07 5 4 3 2

Printed in the United States of America

Cover and book design by Shawn Glidden

Copyedited by Dylan Frautschi

COVER PHOTO: See page 59.

Book Proposals

Iconografix is a publishing company specializing in books for transportation enthusiasts. We publish in a number of different areas, including Automobiles, Auto Racing, Buses, Construction Equipment, Emergency Equipment, Farming Equipment, Railroads & Trucks. The Iconografix imprint is constantly growing and expanding into new subject areas.

Authors, editors, and knowledgeable enthusiasts in the field of transportation history are invited to contact the Editorial Department at Iconografix, Inc., PO Box 446, Hudson, WI 54016.

Acknowledgments

The photos and illustrations in this book are from the holdings of the Ludvigsen Library in London, England. Many of them were gathered by Karl Ludvigsen from the files of Chevrolet when he wrote an article about the Corvair for *Automobile Quarterly*. Stanley Rosenthall took some of the Fitch Sprint and Phoenix photos and those of the racing Corvairs at Sebring and Daytona. Larry Shinoda kindly allowed Ludvigsen to copy some rare photos of the Corvair prototypes and styling models that he co-created with Tony Lapine for Bill Mitchell.

In the 1970s, L. Scott Bailey of *Automobile Quarterly* interviewed Edward Nicholas Cole on the story of the Corvair. Ed Cole was born in Michigan on September 17, 1909 and died there in the crash of a light plane he was piloting in treacherous weather on May 2, 1977. This brilliant, enthusiastic and inspiring engineer contributed to the design of the great Cadillac overhead-valve V-8 of 1949, the immortal Chevrolet V-8 of 1955, and the Corvair—among many other achievements. Ed Cole's was the initiative that led to the removal of lead from fuel and the use of catalysts to cut car emissions. In 1967 he was made president of General Motors, the job from which he retired in 1974.

With the kind permission of both Scott Bailey and Dollie Cole, Ed's widow, this book's Introduction is Ed Cole's first-hand account of the creation and the extinction of the Chevrolet Corvair, one of the most interesting and controversial automobiles ever built. As Dollie Cole put it, "The Corvair is still admired by so many. In this era of high-priced fuel, a Corvair would be the car to own. Safe, comfortable and still stylish. The Corvair deserves better than history remembers it." The Ludvigsen Library hopes that this book will help win many new friends for an exceptionally appealing automobile.

My Corvair Life and Times
by Edward N. Cole

It helps a lot when your work is also your hobby. In the early 1950s the ideas I was tossing about regarding air cooling and rear engines for passenger cars were pretty much a diversion. I was in Cleveland at the time managing Cadillac's tank-manufacturing plant. But my off hours from the plant became increasingly centered in the drafting studio I'd set up in one room of the Lakeshore Hotel in Cleveland. There, with some friends from the plant, we were thinking about new automobiles.

An engineer is rather like a stylist. If he stays on one theme constantly he can go sour. All his thinking becomes channeled. He should explore. Every idea should be put on paper— I believe that is the most orderly way to get the job of thinking done. We developed sketches by the dozens, played with many, many configurations. Among them I began developing sketches for a small rear-engined, air-cooled car. As it happened, these sketches closely resembled the final design of the first Corvairs.

My first real interest in the rear-engined configuration came about earlier than that, around 1945 when I was working with a study project at Cadillac. In 1946 or 1947 we built an experimental rear-engined car, which showed that the concept was technically feasible—but not for a car the size of a Cadillac. As for air cooling, I was introduced to that during World War II with an experimental version of the M-3 light tank powered by a Wright air-cooled engine. We did quite a lot of testing on that particular vehicle and we quickly saw the merits of air cooling for this application.

Then, in 1950, GM was asked by the government to develop a facility to produce another light tank. This was the M-42, and for this we used a 950-cubic-inch supercharged Continental horizontally opposed flat-six. Once more we had exposure to an air-cooled engine—a configuration that was straightforward and simple. Naturally all our engineers working on the project became very familiar with this engine, and we established that it could meet the heavy-duty requirements of a tank very well.

Harry Barr and Kai Hansen had been with me at Cadillac, and when I moved to Chevrolet as chief engineer in 1952, they joined me. From our Lakeshore experience, we already had a pretty good idea of what we wanted to do, and within a few months we started the program which was eventually to produce the Corvair.

There were two elements to this program. First, we saw a definite need for a functional transportation type of vehicle, perhaps smaller than anything that was then available on the American market. This was long before we witnessed the rise of the imports. Imports during the early 1950s were not significant; these small economy cars didn't represent any real volume at that time. Secondly, we could see the benefits that would result from improved technology, which would make a domestic car of this type quite feasible.

We weren't confining ourselves to any specific ideas. When the brilliant British engineer Maurice Olley came to Chevrolet, one of the projects we put to him was the development of the transportation car—one that could do for Americans what the Volkswagen was doing for Europeans. It was a simple statement of the problem and the objective. Naturally we analyzed all the available foreign cars and their configurations and we cost-estimated many of them. I didn't talk to anyone at Porsche, but I did speak to some of the people at Volkswagen; I had known Heinz Nordhoff quite well when he was at GM. And we did have discussions with Henry M. Crane who had formerly been technical adviser to Mr. Sloan when we built several experimental rear-engined cars in the 1930s.

This is where the intrigue comes in, from an engineer's viewpoint. You're faced with a lot of questions and a lot of choices. How would the American buyer take to a new configuration? What are his habits? What does he want? By this time Americans had begun to become acquainted with power assists—to ease steering effort, to get away from the clutch pedal, to brake easier. Locking differentials were coming in, providing an extra tractability advantage. So you put all these things together and you come up with a weight distribution of probably 40/60, forty on the front and sixty on the rear. Then you start working with configurations using rear engines. It gives good braking characteristics, good steering effort. It provides better space distribution within the passenger compartment because you're not fighting tunnels and things of that sort. We filled a large book with many, many studies.

As for air cooling, we firmly believed that this type of engine was absolutely necessary to the success of a competitive lightweight car. It could be made into a compact powerplant in combination with either an automatic transmission or a conventional standard synchromesh. It requires no radiator or cooling system. Also the air used to cool the engine can be directed to heat the passenger compartment.

Edward Nicholas Cole had been general manager of the Chevrolet Motor Division of General Motors for three years when his all-new Corvair was introduced to the press and public in the autumn of 1959. He had good reason to be proud of the radical new car that he and his colleagues had been gestating for a decade.

The air-cooled engine was new to American industry. Much new thinking would have to be done by GM's Manufacturing Staff to produce this type of powerplant in the volume needed to compete in the small-car market. Permanent-mold techniques of producing the engine blocks and cylinder heads appeared ideal for this application, even though a great deal of pioneering work in the casting of aluminum in volume production had to be accomplished by Chevrolet.

Because of its placement the Corvair engine required a low profile, although it was not necessary that it be opposed. But we had been thinking along those lines anyway. Then the question was: should it be a four or a six? From tests we'd done on the four, talks we'd had with engineers at Continental and elsewhere where fours had been built, and our experience with the tank operation, the conclusion came quickly. From the point of view of smoothness and carburetion, the six was easier to handle. And, all things considered, it didn't offer too much of an economic barrier. Everybody voted that the Corvair engine ought to be a six.

A horizontally-opposed six is one of the best-balanced engines in the business from the standpoint of secondary forces and how they are absorbed by adjacent cylinders—whereas in the V-8 you have something of a balance problem in so far as the crankshaft is concerned. The horizontally-opposed six is a very fine engine—as has been proven by aircraft usage. In 1950 I logged about 300 hours in a Continental-powered C Bonanza, flying many times on instruments under unpleasant conditions, and I certainly got to know the great reliability this engine had, and still has for that matter.

We encountered numerous difficulties, as you would expect in any car that has as many completely new components and designs as the Corvair. One of the most frustrating mechanical problems we faced was designing and developing a conventional-looking rear deck lid. This called for a cooling fan that was horizontal. It was a real challenge and the final design was a fan belt with a very unusual drive path. We'd run a good many bench tests on the horizontally-disposed fan. The durability on straight running was good; the thing that was bothersome, that caused some problems, was the mass of the fan during acceleration. The engine had so much power in relation to its flywheel size that its acceleration imposed high forces on the belt which accelerated the impeller—and that's why we went to the lightweight impeller later on, to cut down the acceleration forces.

The second nagging problem we encountered was with the hydraulic tappets. They had to lay in a horizontal position without trapping air and had to be quiet in their operation at all times. However, problems like these only seemed to add to the challenge and excitement of the team of Corvair engineers. My greatest source of encouragement came from these men. They were highly enthusiastic about this new design and confident that it would be an outstanding car. Everybody was more or less on the same wavelength. This is what we wanted to do. *When* we could do it—that was another question.

We had been trying to develop what we thought was the best package. We didn't have any feeling of when we would produce it; we merely proceeded to refine the design so when the need did arise or the corporation thought the project should be pushed, we'd be ready. The project had started to take definite shape in 1954. It was accelerated about 1955, and we decided on the basic configuration for the Corvair in the spring of 1956. It was approved by the corporation as a project for continuing development late in 1957.

There was never any objection or opposition within Chevrolet or General Motors to the Corvair project—quite the contrary. There was general enthusiasm because GM had a new and exciting design concept with which to meet competition in the small-car field. The new concept embodied in the Corvair interested me for a number of reasons, not the least of which was the excitement inherent in exploring new engineering approaches. Equally important was the fact that the results provided many advantages unavailable to other small cars. Among them were maneuverability, traction in mud, snow and ice, easy steering and braking without power assists, a cooler passenger compartment, a flat floor and also a lower profile for a smart styling appearance. Another reason was simply that new and different ideas always stimulate the interest of the American public. This would provide increased showroom traffic of benefit to the sales of all Chevrolet models.

So the Corvair was introduced. The name, by the way, came from a combination of the two most popular names in the Chevrolet line of cars at that time—the Corvette and the Bel Air. The name 'Corvair' was copyrighted by GM following its use on a dream car in the GM Motorama in 1954. The selection of this name was my choice.

During the latter stages in the development of the Corvair— from 1956 on—I was no longer in the engineering department. Everybody gives me a lot of credit for the Corvair—which I like to have—but basically the project was carried through by the engineering people under Harry Barr, who became chief engineer when I moved to general manager. Naturally I had my work cut out for me as general manager at Chevrolet. To get in and really do an engineering job by then wasn't practical—or even possible. But obviously I kept close track of the progress and would go out to the Proving Grounds regularly and drive the results.

Everybody at Chevrolet was pleased with the success of the Corvair project. If there was an area in which it didn't quite come up to expectation it was in the matter of weight. We wanted a basic car for basic transportation with a body frame integrally constructed to conserve weight and at the same time strengthen the structure. We hoped to get the car in the 2,100- 2,200-pound class, as we felt that the economy not only of the material but the fuel consumption and general performance of the car would be enhanced with a smaller and lighter engine if we could achieve the lower weight.

That we didn't achieve the weight we had set out to was somewhat of a disappointment. The Corvair weighed about 150 pounds more than the original designs as a result of modifications to provide greater comfort, visibility and durability. For example, we lengthened the wheelbase six inches to improve leg room in the front compartment. But reasons and results aside, I don't think the extra weight had any bearing on the success or failure of the car.

Throughout our development of the Corvair we had been thinking more of the functional than the sporty, a fact borne out by the late introductory date of the Monza version. Actually our first approach to this car wasn't too well accepted as a pure transportation vehicle. I think we missed the fact that Ameri-

cans wanted a dressed-up car for this sort of thing, something a little more sporty than that with which we first identified the Corvair. As it turned out, of all the Corvair models we built, the two-door Monza was my favorite.

The basic reason for discontinuing the Corvair was declining sales. There were a number of reasons for this, among which were the adverse publicity in the press, the outstanding success of our Chevy II and the apparent demand for more performance from the Corvair. To satisfy the demand for increased performance, it would have been necessary to do major redesign and retooling of the engine and other aspects of the car.

Regarding the engine, there was and has since been considerable speculation about its production cost. While it is true that the use of aluminum in the Corvair engine made it more expensive, there were offsetting factors caused by the simpler design, elimination of the radiator, and so forth. All factors considered, the Corvair engine was competitive in price to engines of similar cars. Cost of the engine definitely was no factor in the discontinuation of the Corvair.

Our Corvair experience was most valuable. The car was intended to be, in effect, the American Volkswagen. We felt it met that need and it could very nicely have continued to fill that slot if it hadn't been attacked vigorously by the critics, and if it had had perhaps a little more tender loving care. But we found ourselves in rather a dilemma. The critic is always right—or his position, at the very least, is considerably stronger than that of the person being put on the defensive.

All in all, we learned a lot from the Corvair. It was a source of both excitement and pride among all those who participated in its development. In looking back, perhaps the greatest thrill for me personally was the first concrete evidence that the Corvair really came up to our hopes and expectations. This came when I test-drove a modified Porsche which contained the new Corvair engine and rear suspension while we were waiting for our first pre-test prototypes of the Corvair to be completed. I drove this car at the GM Technical Center and Milford Proving Grounds in late 1957 and at Pikes Peak, Colorado, in early 1958. She ran beautifully. I knew that we had a winner. I've never changed my mind about that.

Facing Ed Cole, at the end of the table, were some of the architects of his Corvair. Pointing at the drawing with a ruler was Harry Barr, Cole's successor as Chevrolet's chief engineer. Next to him was Ellis "Ed" Premo, in charge of body engineering. On the left was Robert Schilling, responsible for the concept of the Corvair's suspension.

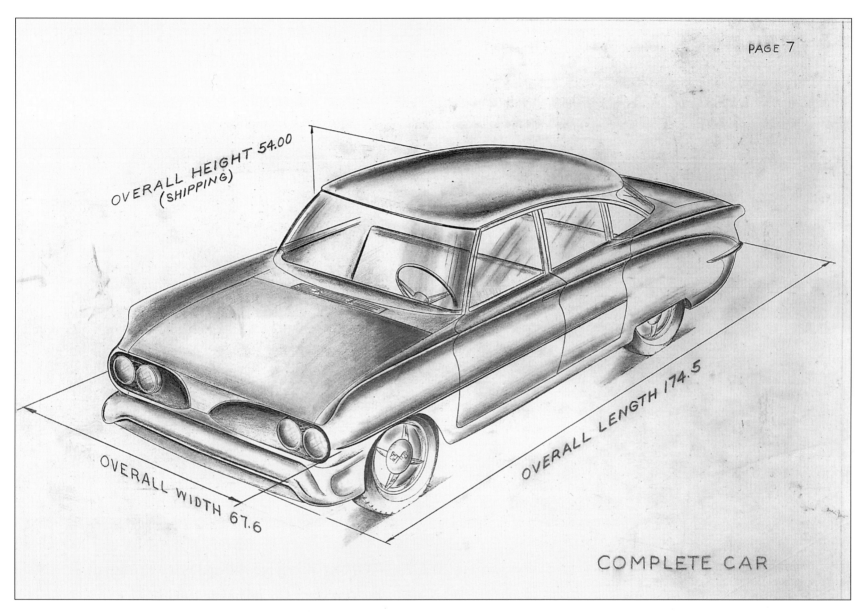

OVERALL HEIGHT 54.00
(SHIPPING)

OVERALL LENGTH 174.5

OVERALL WIDTH 67.6

COMPLETE CAR

A presentation drawing of August 23, 1957 showed styling much more overwrought than that of the eventual Corvair. It resembled more the Pontiac Tempest that would be introduced as a front-engined 1961 model based on the Corvair platform. The ultimate Corvair would be 2.7 inches lower than the concept shown, 0.7 inches narrower and 5.5 inches longer.

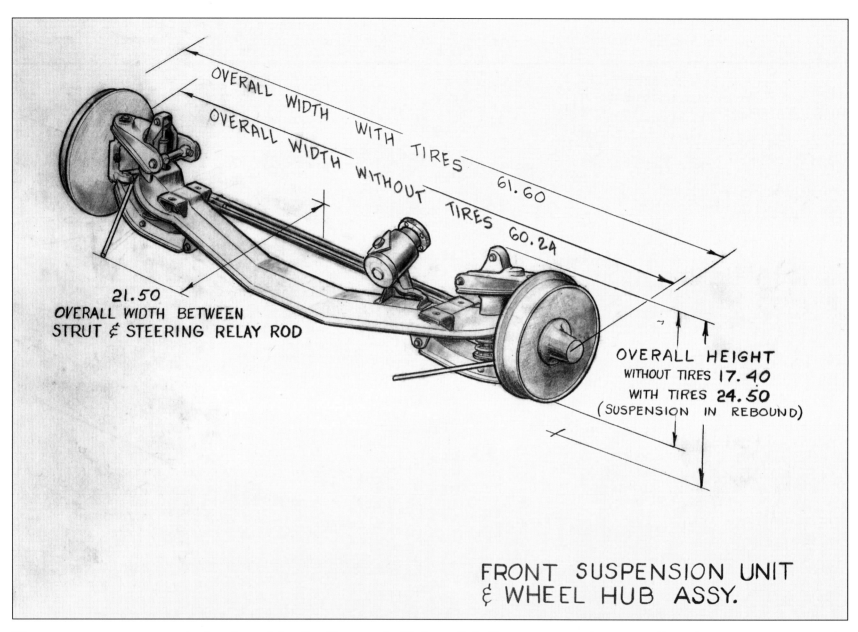

OVERALL WIDTH WITH TIRES 61.60

OVERALL WIDTH WITHOUT TIRES 60.24

21.50
OVERALL WIDTH BETWEEN
STRUT & STEERING RELAY ROD

OVERALL HEIGHT
WITHOUT TIRES 17.40
WITH TIRES 24.50
(SUSPENSION IN REBOUND)

FRONT SUSPENSION UNIT
& WHEEL HUB ASSY.

The suspension concepts developed for the Corvair by Robert Schilling were implemented by Charles Rubly. A 1957 drawing showed the layout of the front suspension, which used upper and lower control arms pivoted from a crossmember that was bolted to the body structure. Springing was by coils.

10

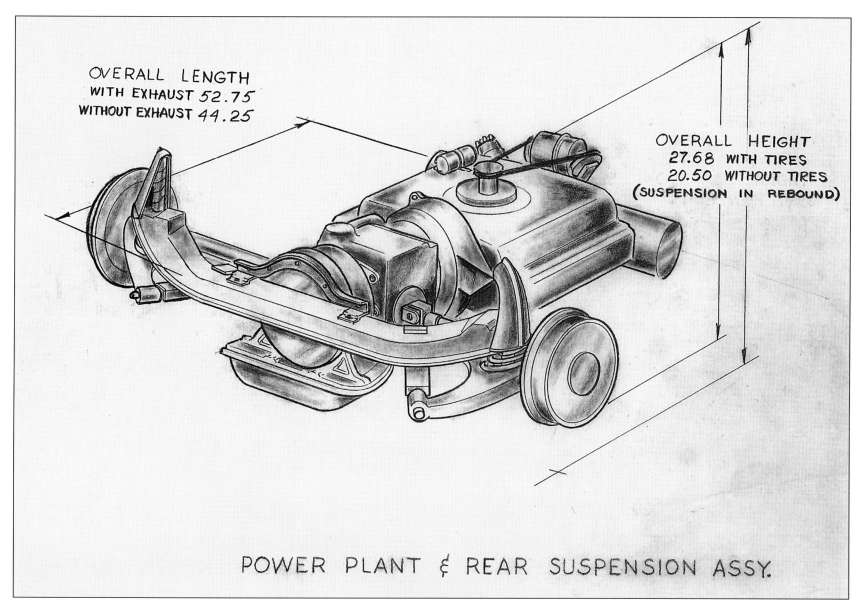

OVERALL LENGTH
WITH EXHAUST 52.75
WITHOUT EXHAUST 44.25

OVERALL HEIGHT
27.68 WITH TIRES
20.50 WITHOUT TIRES
(SUSPENSION IN REBOUND)

POWER PLANT & REAR SUSPENSION ASSY.

Viewed looking towards the rear of the chassis, the Corvair's rear suspension was also mounted to a stamped-steel crossmember. Semi-trailing arms carried each wheel and were sprung by coils. This 1957 concept showed an automatic transmission and the mounting of the generator between the two pulleys that carried the drive from the crankshaft to the horizontal cooling fan.

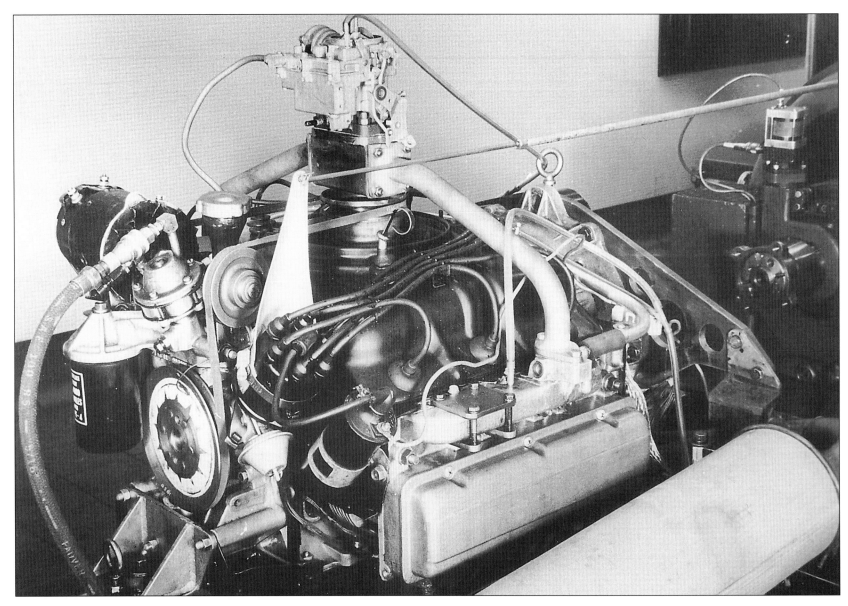

A number of different induction systems were tried during the development of the Corvair's flat-six engine. This experimental installation on a dynamometer at Chevrolet's Engineering Center used a single central carburetor feeding the manifolds in each cylinder head through long, curving downpipes. This arrangement, not unlike that of the Volkswagen, was rejected in favor of a single carburetor for each cylinder bank.

Under test at Chevrolet Engineering in May of 1959 was a Corvair engine equipped with four downdraft carburetors. This became a popular arrangement for those seeking to modify the Corvair to produce more power. Such engines, developed by Zora Arkus-Duntov's performance group at Chevrolet, were used in early racing Corvairs. Four carbs were offered in production by Chevrolet beginning in 1965, producing 140 bhp at 5,200 rpm.

Ed, a Chevrolet technician, gently lowered this prototype Corvair flat-six from the engine bay of the Porsche 356 in which it made its first trips on the road (as mentioned by Ed Cole). Also installed in the Porsche was an early version of the Corvair's trailing-arm rear suspension, sprung by coils instead of the torsion bars used in the Porsche. This installation made use of a manual transmission.

A technician pointed to a row of connectors across the firewall for temperature measurements on the prototype Corvair engine installed in a Porsche 356. This engine had twin carburetors drawing air from a single central cleaner. More than one Porsche was used in the GM test program, evaluating not only the power train but also other chassis elements of the future Corvair. Contrary to many rumors then and later, however, Porsche did not participate in the engineering of the Corvair.

In the newly built Chevrolet Engineering Center at Warren, Michigan, north of Detroit, the body of a Corvair prototype was hand-assembled from provisional parts. Its monocoque structure made use of GM's experience in the design of integral body-frame cars for Opel in Europe. Just after the war, as well, Chevrolet had designed and built prototypes of a "Cadet" small car with an integral body-frame structure.

The body in white for a prototype Corvair neared completion at Chevrolet. Its shape was provisional, because the final styling of the Corvair had yet to be determined. Nevertheless, this particular prototype already showed the wraparound rear window that was such a distinctive feature of the production Corvair.

Components of the prototype Corvair bodies, as here the doors, were hand-fitted by Chevrolet's experts. Massive steel jigs bolted to slotted plates in the floor held all the body components in rigid alignment.

The prototype Corvair body shown on the previous page took to the road to test components. This was a winter test at Duluth in northern Minnesota. An appliqué grille sought to provide the illusion of a front-engined car.

For hot-weather testing of Corvair prototypes Chevrolet used the General Motors Proving Ground at Phoenix, Arizona. This breeze-block enclosure was designed to trap the heat to provide the ultimate extreme trial of stopping and re-starting under high-temperature conditions during a test run. A precisely calibrated fifth wheel was attached to the rear bumper to record exact speeds and distances.

This Corvair prototype had a different roofline than the one shown on the previous pages. It carried "Holden Special" badging, Holden being the GM Australian vehicle range for which Chevrolet had designed several cars. Special "Holden" letterhead was designed and used for the Corvair project, as were Holden purchase orders and engineering drafting paper to preserve security.

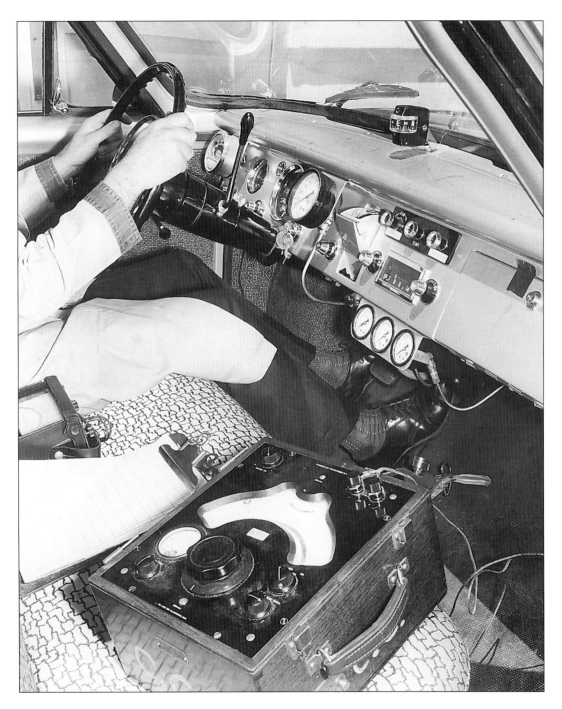

A look inside the cockpit of a Corvair "Holden Special" prototype revealed a wide range of test instrumentation for this automatic-transmission car. Its gear selector was column-mounted. The large test apparatus in the foreground was connected as needed to thermocouples in the engine room and elsewhere to measure component temperatures.

Chevrolet engineer Kai Hansen had much to do with the creation of the Corvair's flat-six engine. Here, suitably garbed for the sub-zero weather in Duluth, Minnesota, Hansen inspected his creation in a "Holden Special." Well into the 1960s one of these black proto-types rested in a parking lot at the GM Technical Center until it was finally scrapped.

At the General Motors Styling Staff, the Corvair's design was carried out under the code designation XP-76. This model of a proposed coupe version was photographed on October 21, 1958. Although many of the eventual design elements were already in place, details still had to be refined.

1961 HOLDEN COUPE

A full-sized airbrush drawing of February 1959 showed the lines proposed for a 1961 "Holden" coupe. The use of the code name continued within GM Styling Staff, although the rendering itself clearly showed the "Corvair" designation. The new car's memorably clean and attractive lines were gradually emerging.

1961 HOLDEN CONV. COUPE

Making use of the same full-sized rendering shown on the previous page, the Chevrolet stylists under Ned Nickels put an alternate top in place to show the way a Corvair convertible would look. The sporty motorist of 1960 would be expected to wear a fedora.

1961 HOLDEN CONV. COUPE

The same rendering was also used to show the proposed appearance with the convertible top erect. Simulated side scoops ahead of the rear wheels would have been appropriate for a rear-engined car but did not survive the final development of the coupe and convertible for production.

By June 1959 a full-sized fiberglass model of a proposed Corvair convertible could be assessed in the viewing yard of GM Styling at Warren, Michigan. Its hubcaps carried the "Chevrolet Corvair" designation. Not until 1962 would this model enter the Corvair range.

A pre-production prototype of the Corvair Club Coupe displayed the elegant simplicity of its lines. The coupes trailed the rest of the Corvair range and were not introduced until January 1960.

In the GM Styling viewing yard a van version of the Corvair, named the Greenbrier, was compared in prototype form with a VW Kombi, on the right, and a British Ford Thames van, on the left. Introduced as a 1961 model, the Greenbrier was dropped from production part way through the 1965 model year. More car-like than van-like, it was much more "roadable" than its rivals.

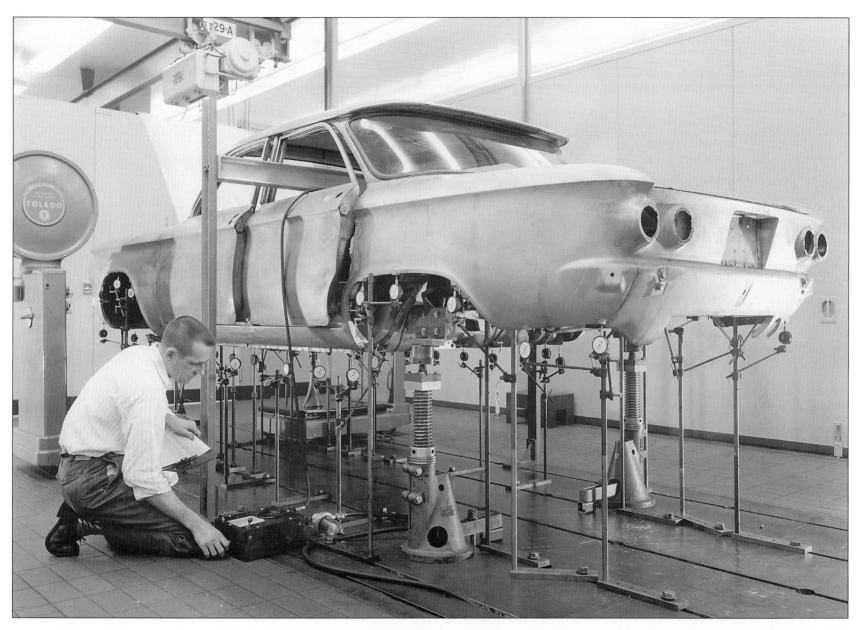

After the final shape of the Corvair was defined, GM's Fisher Body Division took over its preparation for production. This Fisher engineer was setting up a test to determine the stiffness of the body-frame under torsion.

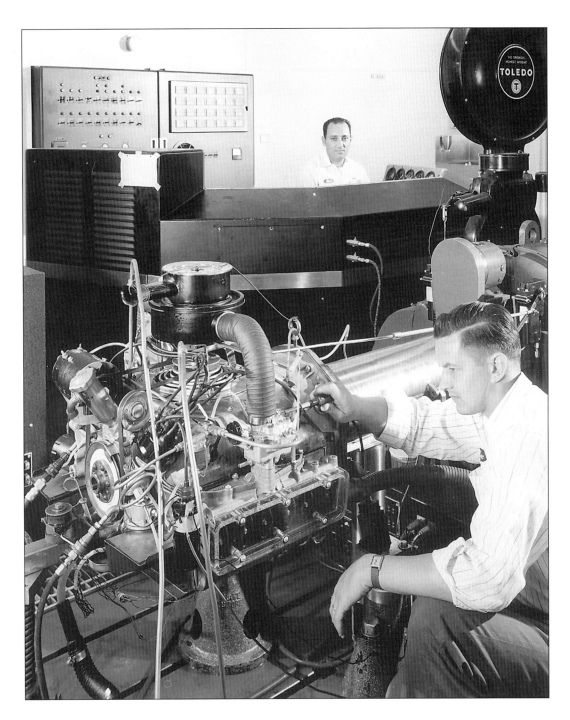

It was four o'clock in the afternoon at Chevrolet Engineering as a technician simulated an adjustment to one of the carburetors of an early prototype Corvair engine. A special Plexiglas cover for the rocker arms allowed the valve gear's lubrication to be studied while the engine was running.

To create a spectacle for Chevrolet's photographers a near-production Corvair engine was run without its exhaust manifolds to show flames belching from the ports. This successfully dramatized the radical nature of Chevrolet's completely new engine.

As seen in plan view, the Corvair six had valves angled away from each other to provide additional space for cooling fins between them. Heads were made of aluminum and the individual cylinders of cast iron. The drive to the camshaft, located below the crankshaft, was taken from the flywheel end of the crank.

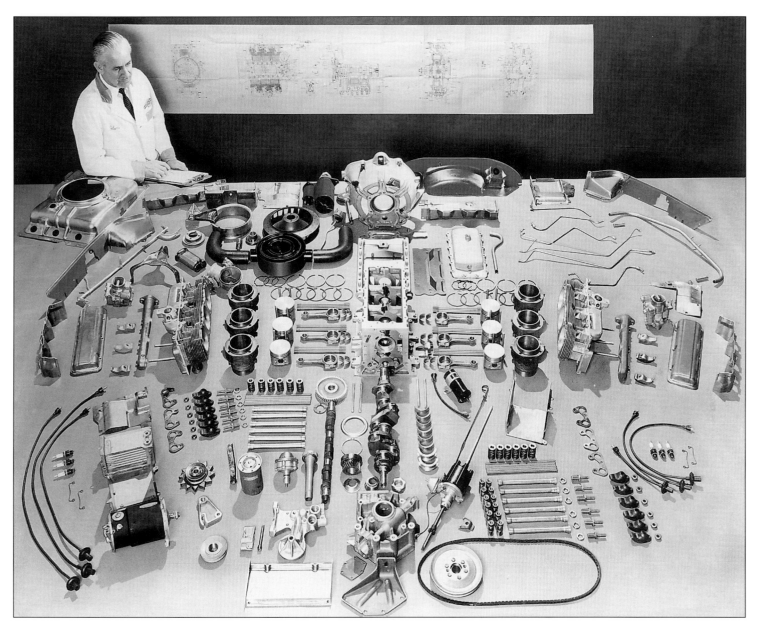

Components of the 1960 Corvair engine were laid out for inspection. It was introduced with the displacement of 140 cubic inches, then enlarged to 145 cubic inches in 1961 by an increase in bore. An unusual feature, dictated by the drive-line arrangement, was that the engine rotated in the opposite sense to all of GM's other power units.

Viewed from the front of the chassis, this Corvair power unit was shown in combination with the rear crossmember and semi-trailing-arm suspension. A forward-facing inlet admitted air to the air cleaner through a single central choke, a feature that was dropped after the 1960 model year. This assembly showed an automatic transmission.

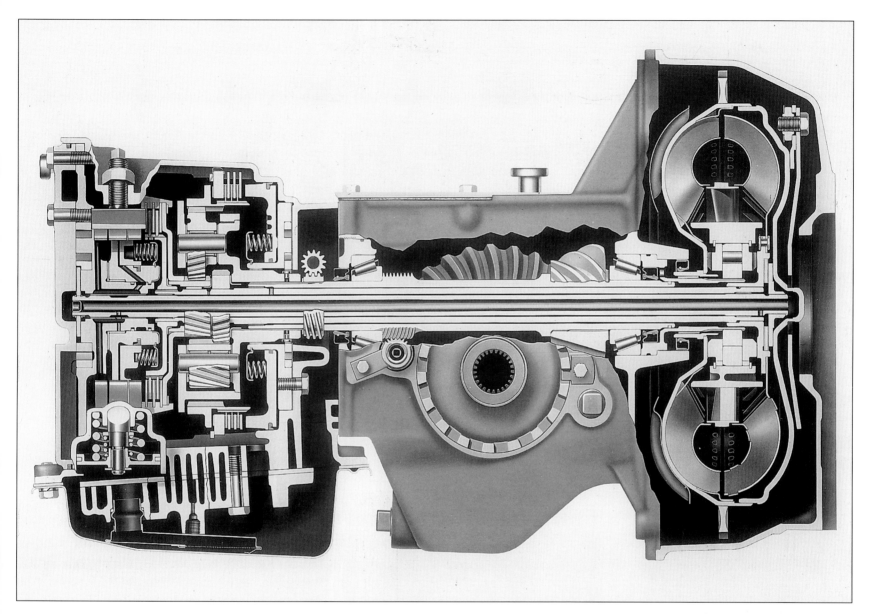

Corvair's Powerglide automatic transmission married a torque converter with a two-speed planetary gear train. A quill shaft drove from the torque converter to the planetary gearbox, inside the shaft that returned to the differential to drive the pinion and ring gear. Ed Cole had hoped that all Corvairs could be automatic but cost pressures forced the addition of manual transmissions to the range—fortunately for car enthusiasts.

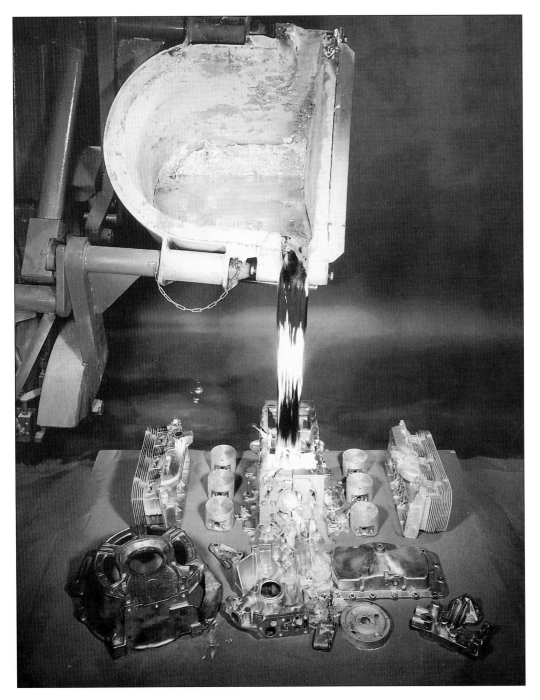

Brilliant Chevrolet public relations man Myron Scott sought to find a way to dramatize how much aluminum was used in the Corvair's engine. In 1960 this lightweight metal was still rare in American-made automobiles. He created this remarkable image of a ladle pouring molten aluminum into the Corvair's cylinder block. The resulting photo was a masterpiece of timing and lighting.

Corvairs were manufactured in the huge factory at Willow Run, west of Detroit, originally built by Ford to produce B-24 bombers during World War II. The factory was then taken over by Kaiser to produce Kaiser and Frazer automobiles. It was completely retooled for manufacture of the Corvair, with Fisher-built bodies carried in cradles for the marriage to them of the front and rear component assemblies.

A pre-production prototype Corvair was photographed in the security of one of GM's proving grounds in preparation for its launch publicity. This car lacked the usual front and side identification. The Corvair rolled on 13-inch wheels fitted with tires especially developed to suit its suspension and weight distribution.

Action photos of the pre-production Corvair highlighted its handsome lines and wraparound rear window giving fine visibility. With bench seating in both front and rear it was rated as a six-passenger model. Its styling, with a high rib line completely encircling the body, was destined to be highly influential.

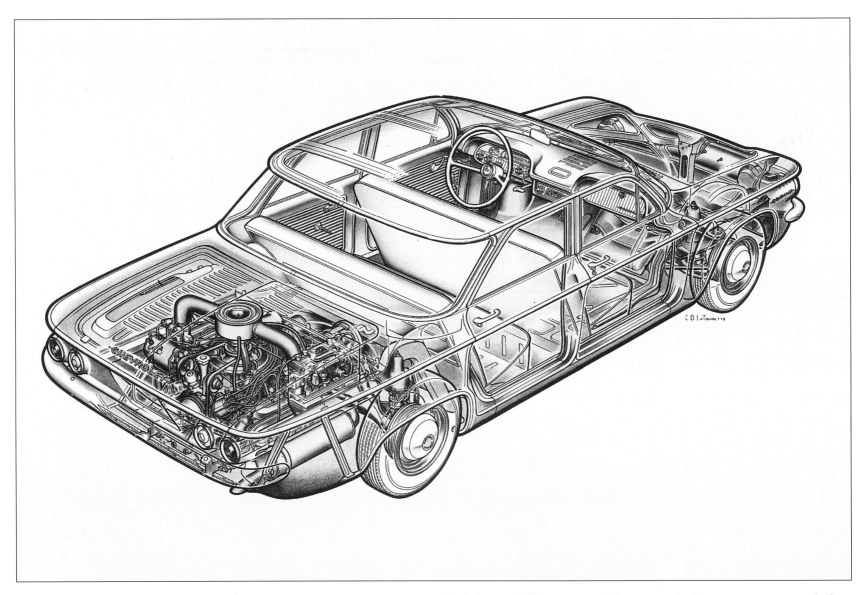

Working from photographs of the Corvair's components, California illustrator Clarence LaTourette created this cutaway drawing of the Corvair. It was published in both the United States and the United Kingdom. It showed the spacious interior and the double-cowled instrument panel, so designed that the Corvair could easily be produced for both right-hand-drive and left-hand-drive markets. An option, later standard on Corvair Monzas, was a forward-folding rear seat back to give more luggage room.

Looking for ways to highlight the Corvair's rear-mounted engine, Chevrolet's Myron Scott hit on the idea of an infrared scanning of the vehicle with its engine running. This image was the result, with the faces of its occupants radiating warmth along with the rear engine compartment.

GM was not slow to promote the merits of its Corvair as a car for Europe. This 700-series four-door Corvair was being assessed by journalists on the continent, together with a Ford Thunderbird. The Corvair had no counterpart among the other cars available in Europe in 1960.

Onlookers at the London Motor Show in 1959 weren't quite sure what to make of this Corvair, fitted as it was with left-hand drive and displayed next to a Corvette. The hood, or "bonnet," has been popped to display the luggage room, much of which was taken up by the spare wheel and the gasoline-fueled heater fitted to early cars.

Chevrolet went to considerable trouble to develop the Lakewood station-wagon version. This Lakewood prototype was photographed in GM Styling's viewing yard on July 10, 1959. The Lakewood was introduced as a 1961 model and dropped from the range in mid-1962, its loss counterbalanced by the introduction of the convertible.

The 1961 Corvair was distinguished by a bulge in its nose that added space to the front luggage compartment. Luggage capacity was further enhanced by the repositioning of the spare under the rear deck. This Corvair sedan carried the chrome trim around its beltline that distinguished the 700-series models from the lesser 500 series.

Narrower whitewalls were the new style trend for 1961. They're featured on this 700-series Corvair Club Coupe, pictured in a nautical setting. Handsome new wheel discs complemented the upscale Corvair models for 1961.

Even a modest 500-series Corvair Club Coupe looked good with its new front trim for 1962, especially when posed in front of a Playboy Club. At $1,992 this was the only Corvair priced under $2,000 in the 1962 model year.

By 1962 the center of gravity of the Corvair range had moved heavily towards the more sporty Monza versions. First introduced in the Club Coupe as the model 900 in May 1960, Monza models had upgraded interior hardware with quality vinyl trim and individual front bucket seats. The introduction of a four-speed manual transmission perfectly complemented these upgrades, as did distinctive wheel-disc designs.

As a GM PR man in 1962, Karl Ludvigsen was asked to stand in for Bill Mitchell to test some photographic setups with a Corvair Monza convertible. Ludvigsen's road test of the original Corvair at its launch in 1959 was one of his first articles as the newly-minted editor of *Sports Cars Illustrated*. Ludvigsen is proud to be an honorary member of the Corvair Society of America.

This 1961 Corvair Monza—identifiable by the badge just forward of the door—was specially trimmed and equipped by GM Styling for one of Bill Mitchell's daughters. The wire wheels gave it added sparkle.

Photographed in the Styling viewing yard on May 19, 1961, the special Monza convertible showed off the pleasing lines of the base vehicle. Its rear was given added character by the four protruding light units, two of them housing concentric reversing lights. Wire wheels became a regular production option for the Corvair in 1962.

March of 1962 saw the introduction of a turbocharged version of the Corvair as an option for the Monza model. Known as the Monza Spyder, it had a dedicated instrument panel with a tachometer, manifold-pressure gauge and a cylinder-head temperature gauge. The turbocharged Spyder engine produced 150 bhp at 4,400 rpm, requiring substantial upgrading of many of its components.

Photographed with the Chevrolet Engineering Center in the background, this 1962 Corvair Monza Spyder looked the epitome of sportiness with its optional wire wheels. It was fitted with non-standard front bumper guards.

The enthusiastic designers at GM Styling couldn't wait to get their hands on the Corvair. Their first radical effort was the Sebring Spyder, introduced in April 1961. Shortened by 18 inches, the car's fiberglass rear deck lifted to show luggage space between its seats and the engine. Side scoops for the rear brakes were functional and its exhaust pipes emerged behind the rear wheels. It was given added power by a Paxton centrifugal supercharger.

On July 12, 1961 GM Styling wheeled out the Sebring Spyder for a gathering of Corvair enthusiasts at the beautiful General Motors Technical Center in Warren, Michigan. Leaning against the car was the head of GM Styling, William L. Mitchell, and next to him was chief Chevrolet designer Clare MacKichan. Neil Madler's photo showed the Corvairs in a serried rank in front of the GM Styling building.

In advance of the introduction of the 1962 Monza Spyder GM's designers produced this coupe based on a 1961 model, which carried the Spyder identification and a decorative scoop feature on its flanks. Its wire wheels, bucket seats and paint scheme adapted from the Sebring Spyder gave it looks to match its turbocharged engine.

Featured here and on the cover, another variation on the Corvair minus a foot and a half of wheelbase is the Super Spyder of 1962, the creation of Larry Shinoda working with Bill Mitchell. This achieved a consummately successful adaptation of the basic shape of the Corvair to a strikingly handsome and original front end. The Super Spyder rolled on aluminum Hands wheels with three-eared knock-off caps.

Not all adaptations of the Corvair were sporty. GM used the Corvair as a basis for its "Calvair," a vehicle powered by a Stirling engine which drew heat from a stored supply—thus the "Cal" for "calories." Bizarrely the GM Research engineers equipped this unique fastback Corvair with optional wire-wheel trim covers.

General Motors used the original Corvair for electric-car experiments in the mid-1960s, creating the "Electrovair." In 1968 a team of students at the Massachusetts Institute of Technology used a later-model Corvair as the basis of a competitor in a transcontinental electric car race. Its nose was modified to improve its aerodynamics.

The MIT students packed their modified Corvair with exotic controlling and charging gear and high-tech batteries. These experimental systems naturally suffered their fair share of problems in the transcontinental race of 1968.

In a cockpit whose complexity recalled that of the "Holden" prototype shown earlier, MIT's electric Corvair had batteries of switches, knobs and indicators. They assisted in monitoring and controlling the car's systems.

No one was quicker to grasp and exploit the sporty potential of the Corvair than former racing driver John Fitch. In these premises at Lakeville, Connecticut, not far from his home in Lime Rock, Fitch and his crew engineered and built the modifications that turned a Corvair into a Fitch Sprint. A Fitch conversion of an early Monza was in the foreground while a later model was at right.

Fitch had the ingenious idea of fitting a stone guard to the front of the Corvair to give his Sprints a distinctive appearance. He speeded up both the steering and shifting and fitted a four-carburetor engine with open exhausts capable of 155 bhp. A vinyl-covered padded roof completed the ensemble, which was priced all-inclusive at $2,995.

With its many advancements in the speed and style of its standard Corvair, Chevrolet presented John Fitch with a moving target. Thus he decided to create a car of his own, making use of a Corvair engine and suspension components, much in the style of the then-popular dune buggies and other vehicles using Volkswagen running gear. Gerald Mong, designer and builder of Bobsy sports-racing cars, designed a fabricated sheet-steel frame to carry the Corvair pieces on a 95-inch wheelbase, 13 inches shorter than standard. Although originally completed early in 1964, the frame was later altered to accommodate the new suspension components that Chevrolet introduced for the 1965 Corvair.

Fitch initially conceived his "Super Sprint" as a light fiberglass-bodied vehicle that could be driven either as a sports car or with its fenders removed as a racing car. Suitable designs were prepared by his friend and long-time collaborator, illustrator and car enthusiast Coby Whitmore.

From the "Super Sprint" concept Fitch's Corvair-based car evolved into his much more elaborate Phoenix. It retained Whitmore's genial concept of side-mounted spare wheels. The Phoenix could also be ordered with a single spare under the front deck. In this configuration the former spare-wheel containers could hold luggage.

The body for the Phoenix was built in Turin, Italy, by Frank Reisner's Carrozzeria Intermeccanica. The Phoenix incorporated a Targa-type roof and a rear window that opened electrically for added ventilation.

Under the rear deck of the Phoenix was a Corvair six of 164 cubic inches (2,688 cc) developing 160 bhp at 5,000 rpm. Italian Weber carburetors were also offered to provide an added 10 bhp.

Fitch's Phoenix had a handsome cockpit with a 6,000-rpm tachometer and 140 mph speedometer. Its top speed, he said, would exceed 130 mph and acceleration from 0-60 would be in 7.5 seconds. Placing of minor switchgear was haphazard in the time-honored style of Italian custom coachbuilders.

The Phoenix by Fitch had a glamorous introduction at New York sporting-goods store Abercrombie & Fitch (no relation) on July 7, 1966. While his original vision for the Super Sprint had been a price of $3,800, Fitch exchanged the digits to announce a price of $8,300 for the Phoenix. His expectation was for sales of some 500 units in its first year. Service of the Corvair-based Phoenix was to be by Chevrolet dealers.

Although a gorgeous automobile, the Fitch Phoenix was fated not to enter production. Ironically this was due to the account of the components that had inspired its creation. Just when the Phoenix was launched, the Corvair was coming under heavy criticism from advocates of improved automotive safety. Although the Corvair's design would ultimately be vindicated by the Federal authorities and the courts, Fitch realized that it would be an uphill battle to fight the prejudice that the publicity aimed at the Corvair. John Fitch remained the sole owner of a Phoenix.

General Motors and Turin coachbuilder Pininfarina enjoyed a friendly relationship; Pininfarina had produced limited series of Eldorados for Cadillac in the late 1950s. On a Corvair chassis donated by GM, Pininfarina produced this elegant two-door coupe for the 1961 European motor shows. Its front end was Porsche-like.

In 1962 Pininfarina took a second cut at the Corvair, with this attractive result. This car had a more distinctive front-end design and a more balanced line than its 1961 predecessor. It hinted strongly at what a future Corvair could look like. Its airy and elegantly shaped greenhouse could not help influencing the GM designers who were already thinking about the next Corvair.

Under the benevolent direction of studio chief Ed Wayne, Larry Shinoda, left, and Anatole "Tony" Lapine created car designs for Bill Mitchell in a semi-secret basement studio. Here they have come up for air to display, in the Styling Staff viewing dome, a space buck and a clay model of a sports car using Corvair components. Like others, they too were eager to exploit the opportunity offered by GM's radical new automobile.

By the time this photo of the clay model was taken by Neil Madler on May 4, 1962, the running version of the car derived from it, the Corvair Monza GT, was virtually complete. The Monza GT was built on a chassis supplied by Chevrolet Engineering, which had its engine mid-mounted ahead of the rear wheels.

The Corvair Monza GT was a magnificent-looking sports car, an unabashed indication that if General Motors wished to put such a car on the road, it could do so with ease. The headlamps of the GT were hidden behind clamshell doors that opened and closed electrically.

As a sister to the GT coupe, GM Styling built the Monza SS Roadster. This delightful two-seater had its engine mounted in the conventional Corvair position, behind the rear axle. It also featured "theater seating," a spring-loaded seat which slid upward under the driver and passenger as they exited the car.

A lift-up canopy of the type used on the Corvair Monza GT was a novelty at the car's first appearance at Elkhart Lake, Wisconsin, in June of 1962. The GT made several such appearances, including one at Watkins Glen, before it was formally introduced to the public, as here at the 1963 Turin Salon. The full functionality of its rear air-inlet grilles is evident.

The chassis on which the Monza GT was built originated at Chevrolet Engineering under its research and development director Frank Winchell and engineer Jim Musser. It had parallel-wishbone front and rear suspension with springing by torsion bars. Braking was by discs. The GT is shown in 1964 (now with properly styled exterior-mirror housings) in the mechanical assembly room inside GM Styling Staff.

As Spartan as sports cars should be, the cockpit of the Monza GT was trimmed in silver to match its exterior. Its steering wheel was quick-detachable to ease entry and exit. Lap belts retracted into the sides of the seats.

The frame structure of the Corvair Monza GT rose high at the rear to encase the engine, much like that of the later Lancia Stratos. Although the GT was originally powered by an experimental flat-six with individual cylinder and head assemblies, when it was sent abroad for motor shows a more conventional Corvair engine was fitted.

At the 1963 Turin Salon the Corvair Monza GT was displayed on the stand of Opel, GM's European subsidiary. Its pillarless wraparound windscreen gave the driver a fabulous sense of visibility and ease of positioning the rapid little coupe on the road. This was much appreciated by the European journalists who had a chance to drive the GT.

English photographer Edward Eves captured some of the interest that Italians showed in the Corvair Monza GT at the 1963 Turin show. One of the car's innovations was Larry Shinoda's use of louvers for the rear window, which in this case could be opened or closed. This influenced the design of future Italian sports cars such as the Lamborghini Miura and the Lancia Stratos.

Bill Mitchell and his designers in the basement studio were well aware that the odds were heavily against the possibility of Chevrolet producing something like the Monza GT, but that didn't keep them from trying. They styled a version that could be built on a shortened Corvair chassis with the engine in its usual rearward location. Although given conventional doors, pillars and headlamps, it retained much of the flair of the original Monza GT.

Based on the Corvair Monza SS, the potential of a roadster version of the car was explored. This model was taken outside for viewing in June of 1963. Unlike many such studies it even found room for a front license plate.

As a close-coupled convertible the Monza GT/SS concept still had a lot to offer. Its concave tail and four lighting units remained true to the Corvair from which its components originated. A means of providing its tail with bumper protection was being evaluated.

Even in the basement studio at GM Styling Staff the roadable roadster version of the Monza SS made a powerfully positive impression. Shinoda and Lapine had done their work well. For Chevrolet, however, one sports car at a time was enough, and in 1963 the new Corvette Stingray was that sports car.

At the Geneva Salon in March 1963 Bertone unveiled its Testudo, a concept car built on a Corvair platform. Its appearance was a shock and a surprise to GM's designers, who had given visitors from Bertone a glimpse of the Monza GT during a visit to Detroit. They felt—not without good reason—that the Testudo's lift-up canopy was a straight steal from the Monza GT. Although their car's name meant "tortoise," Bertone's designers had not been slow in exploiting an attractive new theme.

Larry Shinoda, right, and Ron Hill inspected a full-size drawing of another sports-car concept intended to make use of Corvair components. Talented Californian Hill was tapped to run the studio responsible for creating a successor to the original Corvair, working under Henry Haga and Bill Mitchell.

GM's designers faced a major challenge in their efforts to update the Corvair for 1965. Chevrolet had introduced its angular Chevy II as a companion car in the same category to make a direct attack on Ford's Falcon. Thus the Corvair had to move in a more sculptured and sporty direction as this October 1962 study suggested.

In their early studies for the 1965 Corvair GM's stylists were trying to keep the prominent beltline which was such a successful feature of the original design. In this study they married it to an aggressive front-end profile.

Given a plastic skin that simulated paint, this Corvair clay model of November 1962 was a further evolution of the design shown on the previous pages. The designers also tried forms that had prominent bulges in their fenders for jounce above the wheels.

A study of September 1962 conveyed a look that was heavier and more imposing than that of the original car. A prominent ridge along the beltline was still a distinctive feature of its design, echoing the original 1960 style.

Dean Zeeb photographed this handsome proposal for a 1965 Corvair on November 5, 1962. Its design was heavily influenced by that of the Monza GT, especially its concave tail and quadruple taillights.

fluenced as it was by the Monza GT, this design proposal for a 1965 Corvair Coupe had no sign of the prominent ncircling rib that characterized the previous model. Its front end, however, was very close to that of the 1965 model.

By February 1963 the shape of the 1965 Corvair sedan was emerging. With a high break line along its fenders offered only a hint of the original Corvair's prominent encircling rib. Traces of the Monza GT are still to be see in the design of its tail.

In near-final form as photographed on February 5, 1963 by Dean Zeeb, the clay model of the 1965 Corvair showed a handsome sedan, albeit lacking the distinctive character of the 1960-1964 model. Chevrolet's designers and managers had decided on a direction that was more conservative than radical.

A final prototype of the 1965 Corvair Monza Spyder Sport Coupe was photographed in one of the spacious hallways of GM Styling Staff in February 1964. The name "Spyder" was in fact used on only a few of the early 1965 production cars fitted with the optional turbocharged engine developing 180 bhp at 4,000 rpm.

In July 1965 a Corvair Monza Sport Coupe was wheeled out to the Styling viewing yard for a nose-to-tail comparison with a fiberglass model of the Chevrolet Camaro then under development. Both cars exhibited the high level of mastery of form achieved by GM's designers working under Bill Mitchell. The glassy greenhouse of the Corvair contrasted with the more enclosed look of the Camaro.

The artists at Chevrolet's PR department made clever use of a fork-lift truck and heavy retouching to compare a 1964 Monza Sedan with a 1965 Monza Sports Sedan. The new model was three inches longer than its predecessor and over two inches wider. It conveyed a more elegant and sedate impression than its cheeky forebear.

When a 1967 Corvair Monza Sports Sedan was photographed on GM Styling's viewing road at the Technical Center, the model's positioning was not by chance. She dramatized the pillarless design of the late-model Corvair, a feature of both sedan and coupe. The year 1967 was the last year of production for the sedan, which accounted for 6,116 of a total of 27,253 1967-model Corvairs—a dramatic drop from 103,743 in 1966 and 235,528 in 1965.

In 1964 the stroke of the Corvair engine had been increased to 2.94 inches, which, with a bore of 3.44 inches, enlarged its displacement to 164 cubic inches. In 1965 an alternator replaced the original generator. This was the base engine, developing 95 bhp at 3,600 rpm. With a compression ratio of 9.25:1 instead of 8.25:1, this engine produced 110 bhp at 4,400 rpm.

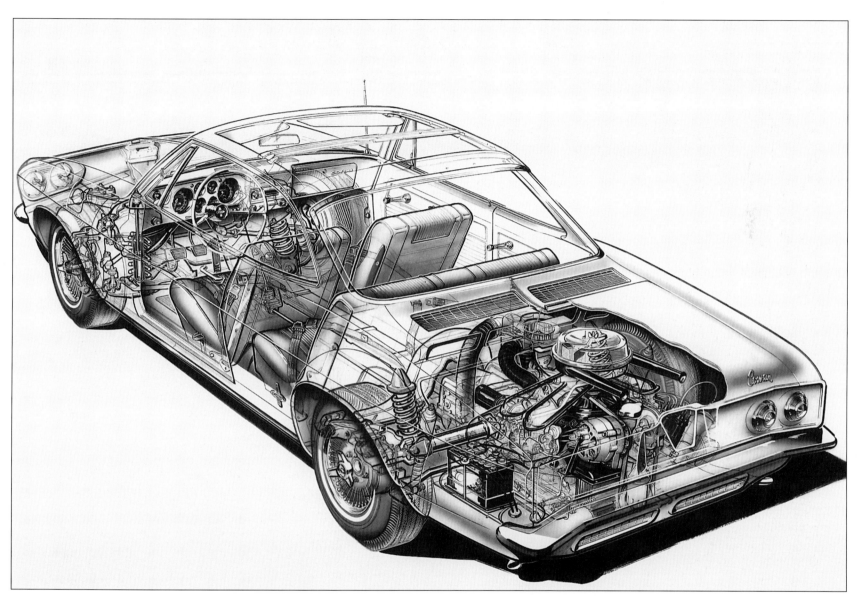

A cutaway drawing by Leslie Luff showed the engineering of the new-generation Corvair, in this case a Corsa Sport Coupe equipped with the four-carburetor 140-bhp engine. Derived from that of the Corvette, its new rear suspension used the drive shaft as one of the links of a parallel-arm guidance for the rear-wheel hubs.

The elegant lines of the 1965 Corvair were displayed in their simplest and least-adorned form on the base 500-series Coupe and Sedan model. A three-speed transmission was standard and a four-speed was optional, together with Chevrolet's Powerglide automatic transmission.

At a special showing of GM's 1965 models on the continent, Briton Edward Eves photographed this 1965 Corvair Monza Sport Coupe. It looked right at home in its European surroundings.

Curious faces peered through the railings as Chevrolet's photographer captured a 1966 Corvair Corsa Sport Coupe for posterity. An attractive new model, the Corsa was distinguished by argent paint in the cove at the rear of the body and an exceptionally handsome six-gauge instrument package. In the Corsa models the 140-bhp engine was standard and the 180-bhp turbocharged six was an option.

Especially when presented as a 1966 Corsa model, the second-generation Corvair Sport Coupe qualified as one of the prettiest cars ever produced. Its lines were excellent and its pillarless greenhouse subtly refined. Its proportions did not attempt to belie the fact that its engine was rear-mounted.

As a curtain-raiser to their 1965 12-hour race the Sebring, Florida, organizers staged a three-hour race for Group 2 FIA sedans. The race attracted international attention with a factory team of five BMW sedans, two of which surrounded a 1965 Corvair Corsa Sport Coupe on the starting grid.

The turbocharged Corvair Corsa was entered at Sebring by Detroit's Don Eichstaedt, who shipped it by air to the Tampa, Florida, airport. The Corsa's wide rear tires gave an indication of the extra horsepower that Eichstaedt had extracted from the car's turbocharged engine.

The interior of Don Eichstaedt's race-prepared Corvair showed its standard Corsa steering wheel and gauge package plus three extra gauges to monitor temperatures and pressures. A racing seat was installed, as was a leftward extension to the accelerator pedal to permit heel-and-toe downshifting.

At the start of the 1965 three-hour race at Sebring, which was run over a shortened version of the circuit, the Corvair surged into the lead. It was soon overtaken by the Lotus Cortinas of Jim Clark and Jack Sears, who finished first and second. Not yet fully developed, the high-pressure Corvair didn't figure in the final result.

In 1965 a Chevrolet dealer in Canonsburg, Pennsylvania, began modifying Corvair Sport Coupes to create the two-seat Yenko Stinger sports car. Yenko Chevrolet ultimately produced 185 Stingers. This Stinger was driven in the 1966 Daytona 24-hour race by Russ MacGrotty and Art Riley. An oil cooler was mounted above its rear deck.

At Daytona the MacGrotty/Riley Stinger was caught by photographer Stanley Rosenthall between a Triumph and the winning Ford GT Mark II of Ken Miles and Lloyd Ruby. The Stinger fell to 40th place in the race during repairs to a broken throttle rod but recovered to place 27th of 32 finishers. Accepted in the SCCA's D Production category, Stingers enjoyed great success and continue to be raced at this writing. Stingers were offered in stages of tune of 160, 190, 200 and 240 bhp, the last achieved by enlarging the displacement from 164 to 176 cubic inches.

After the 1965 Corvair's styling had been frozen, GM's designers continued to explore alternatives for the design of future models. This coupe proposal took the Corvair's design in a significantly more sporty direction. It soon became evident, however, that under its new general manager, Elliott "Pete" Estes, Chevrolet did not intend to develop the Corvair. Production from 1967 through 1969, maintains historian Tony Fiore, was prolonged chiefly to avoid criticism of a too-sudden dropping of the model in the face of Ralph Nader's assault on its safety.

A study of July 1964 suggested the evolution of the Corvair in a more massive direction, with a fastback greenhouse. The theme of air scoops in the rear fender panels, often explored earlier, was revived for this proposal.

In 1965 Chevrolet's engineers installed a V-8 engine of 287 cubic inches in the rear of a Corvair Sport Coupe, driving through a modified Pontiac Tempest transaxle. Its aluminum radiators were mounted in the rear. As many private V-8 engine installations have subsequently shown, this was happily accommodated by the Corvair. A GM designer's sketch of August 24, 1964 suggested a possible front-end appearance for a V-8-powered Corvair.

A purposeful rear-end proposal for a future Corvair was sketched by a GM designer at a time when it was still hoped that the auto could be kept alive. This was not to be, however. The final model year for the Corvair was 1969, with only 6,000 coupes and convertibles produced. Up to the building of the last car on October 29, 1969 total Corvair production over its decade-long life amounted to 1,787,243.

Like its designers, Chevrolet's engineers were reluctant to give up on the Corvair. In the mid-1960s they developed a new Porsche-like engine with a single overhead camshaft for each cylinder bank operating inclined valves through rocker arms. The cams were driven by cogged rubber belts. Each opposing pair of cylinders was cooled by its own centrifugal blower. Triple-bodied carburetors were fitted to this exciting engine, designed to a potential of 240 bhp at 7,200 rpm. Before it could be perfected, however, all Corvair development was stopped. Sadly, this gorgeous engine never powered a car.

As a successor to the Monza GT, Chevrolet's stylists sought to produce an even lower and wilder show car. These renderings of their ultra-low design proposals were recorded on January 25, 1966. One designer aptly titled his submission "Panther."

Evolved from the design sketches on the preceding page, the Chevrolet Astro I concept car took shape in the fabrication shops of GM Styling Staff. Based on another experimental chassis from Chevrolet Research and Development, it rolled on 13-inch magnesium wheels. Inlets below the nose were for front-brake cooling and the rear-view mirror was periscopic. Finished in red, the Astro I had its debut at the 1967 New York Show.

Overall height of the stunning Astro I was only 35 1/2 inches. For entry its rear canopy hinged upward, bringing the individual bucket seats with it. Occupants settled into the seats, which then slid back into position as the canopy was closed electrically. The engine was mounted behind the rear wheels, as in the standard model. In their efforts to produce an ultimate Corvair, Chevrolet's designers and engineers had done very well indeed.

Countless Corvairs have been modified for show and go by enthusiasts. None has matched the astonishing conversion achieved by California engineer Jay Eitel. Its standard post-1965 rear suspension was connected to a special rear transaxle produced by Pontiac for racing of its Tempest model. This rear assembly, with its finned oil pan, was driven from a front-mounted engine through a drive shaft running in a rigid tube.

In the trunk of his Corvair Eitel installed a V-12 Jaguar engine, each bank of cylinders fed by its own fuel-injection system. Cooled by blowers, the radiator for the engine was mounted in the rear of Eitel's Corvair. The engineer designed his Corvair's exhaust system so that the vehicle, completely standard externally, even sounded like a six-cylinder Corvair. His must be considered one of the ultimate tributes to a fine automobile design.

MORE TITLES FROM ICONOGRAFIX:

AMERICAN CULTURE

AMERICAN SERVICE STATIONS 1935-1943 PHOTO ARCHIVE	ISBN 1-882256-27-1
COCA-COLA: A HISTORY IN PHOTOGRAPHS 1930-1969	ISBN 1-882256-46-8
COCA-COLA: ITS VEHICLES IN PHOTOGRAPHS 1930-1969	ISBN 1-882256-47-6
PHILLIPS 66 1945-1954 PHOTO ARCHIVE	ISBN 1-882256-42-5

AUTOMOTIVE

CADILLAC 1948-1964 PHOTO ALBUM	ISBN 1-882256-83-2
CAMARO 1967-2000 PHOTO ARCHIVE	ISBN 1-58388-032-1
CLASSIC AMERICAN LIMOUSINES 1955-2000 PHOTO ARCHIVE	ISBN 1-58388-041-0
CORVAIR by CHEVROLET EXP. & PROD. CARS 1957-1969 LUDVIGSEN LIBRARY SERIES	ISBN 1-58388-058-5
CORVETTE THE EXOTIC EXPERIMENTAL CARS, LUDVIGSEN LIBRARY SERIES	ISBN 1-58388-017-8
CORVETTE PROTOTYPES & SHOW CARS PHOTO ALBUM	ISBN 1-882256-77-8
EARLY FORD V-8S 1932-1942 PHOTO ALBUM	ISBN 1-882256-97-2
IMPERIAL 1955-1963 PHOTO ARCHIVE	ISBN 1-882256-22-0
IMPERIAL 1964-1968 PHOTO ARCHIVE	ISBN 1-882256-23-9
LINCOLN MOTOR CARS 1920-1942 PHOTO ARCHIVE	ISBN 1-882256-57-3
LINCOLN MOTOR CARS 1946-1960 PHOTO ARCHIVE	ISBN 1-882256-58-1
PACKARD MOTOR CARS 1935-1942 PHOTO ARCHIVE	ISBN 1-882256-44-1
PACKARD MOTOR CARS 1946-1958 PHOTO ARCHIVE	ISBN 1-882256-45-X
PONTIAC DREAM CARS, SHOW CARS & PROTOTYPES 1928-1998 PHOTO ALBUM	ISBN 1-882256-93-X
PONTIAC FIREBIRD TRANS-AM 1969-1999 PHOTO ALBUM	ISBN 1-882256-95-6
PONTIAC FIREBIRD 1967-2000 PHOTO HISTORY	ISBN 1-58388-028-3
STUDEBAKER 1933-1942 PHOTO ARCHIVE	ISBN 1-882256-24-7
ULTIMATE CORVETTE TRIVIA CHALLENGE	ISBN 1-58388-035-6

BUSES

BUSES OF MOTOR COACH INDUSTRIES 1932-2000 PHOTO ARCHIVE	ISBN 1-58388-039-9
FLXIBLE TRANSIT BUSES 1953-1995 PHOTO ARCHIVE	ISBN 1-58388-053-4
THE GENERAL MOTORS NEW LOOK BUS PHOTO ARCHIVE	ISBN 1-58388-007-0
GREYHOUND BUSES 1914-2000 PHOTO ARCHIVE	ISBN 1-58388-027-5
*MACK® BUSES 1900-1960 PHOTO ARCHIVE**	ISBN 1-58388-020-8
TRAILWAYS BUSES 1936-2001 PHOTO ARCHIVE	ISBN 1-58388-029-1
TROLLEY BUSES 1913-2001 PHOTO ARCHIVE	ISBN 1-58388-057-7
YELLOW COACH BUSES 1923-1943 PHOTO ARCHIVE	ISBN 1-58388-054-2

EMERGENCY VEHICLES

AMERICAN LAFRANCE 700 SERIES 1945-1952 PHOTO ARCHIVE	ISBN 1-882256-90-5
AMERICAN LAFRANCE 700 SERIES 1945-1952 PHOTO ARCHIVE VOLUME 2	ISBN 1-58388-025-9
AMERICAN LAFRANCE 700 & 800 SERIES 1953-1958 PHOTO ARCHIVE	ISBN 1-882256-91-3
AMERICAN LAFRANCE 900 SERIES 1958-1964 PHOTO ARCHIVE	ISBN 1-58388-002-X
CROWN FIRECOACH 1951-1985 PHOTO ARCHIVE	ISBN 1-58388-047-X
CLASSIC AMERICAN AMBULANCES 1900-1979 PHOTO ARCHIVE	ISBN 1-882256-94-8
CLASSIC AMERICAN FUNERAL VEHICLES 1900-1980 PHOTO ARCHIVE	ISBN 1-58388-016-X
CLASSIC SEAGRAVE 1935-1951 PHOTO ARCHIVE	ISBN 1-58388-034-8
FIRE CHIEF CARS 1900-1997 PHOTO ALBUM	ISBN 1-882256-87-5
HEAVY RESCUE TRUCKS 1931-2000 PHOTO GALLERY	ISBN 1-58388-045-3
INDUSTRIAL AND PRIVATE FIRE APPARATUS 1925-2001 PHOTO ARCHIVE	ISBN 1-58388-049-6
LOS ANGELES CITY FIRE APPARATUS 1953 - 1999 PHOTO ARCHIVE	ISBN 1-58388-012-7
*MACK MODEL C FIRE TRUCKS 1957-1967 PHOTO ARCHIVE**	ISBN 1-58388-014-3
*MACK MODEL CF FIRE TRUCKS 1967-1981 PHOTO ARCHIVE**	ISBN 1-882256-63-8
*MACK MODEL L FIRE TRUCKS 1940-1954 PHOTO ARCHIVE**	ISBN 1-882256-86-7
MAXIM FIRE APPARATUS 1914-1989 PHOTO ARCHIVE	ISBN 1-58388-050-X
NAVY & MARINE CORPS FIRE APPARATUS 1836 -2000 PHOTO GALLERY	ISBN 1-58388-031-3
PIERCE ARROW FIRE APPARATUS 1979-1998 PHOTO ARCHIVE	ISBN 1-58388-023-2
POLICE CARS: RESTORING, COLLECTING & SHOWING AMERICA'S FINEST SEDANS	ISBN 1-58388-046-1
SEAGRAVE 70TH ANNIVERSARY SERIES PHOTO ARCHIVE	ISBN 1-58388-001-1
VOLUNTEER & RURAL FIRE APPARATUS PHOTO GALLERY	ISBN 1-58388-005-4
WARD LAFRANCE FIRE TRUCKS 1918-1978 PHOTO ARCHIVE	ISBN 1-58388-013-5
WILDLAND FIRE APPARATUS 1940-2001 PHOTO GALLERY	ISBN 1-58388-056-9
YOUNG FIRE EQUIPMENT 1932-1991 PHOTO ARCHIVE	ISBN 1-58388-015-1

RACING

EL MIRAGE IMPRESSIONS: DRY LAKES LAND SPEED RACING	ISBN 1-58388-059-3
GT40 PHOTO ARCHIVE	ISBN 1-882256-64-6
INDY CARS OF THE 1950s, LUDVIGSEN LIBRARY SERIES	ISBN 1-58388-018-6
INDY CARS OF THE 1960s, LUDVIGSEN LIBRARY SERIES	ISBN 1-58388-052-6
INDIANAPOLIS RACING CARS OF FRANK KURTIS 1941-1963 PHOTO ARCHIVE	ISBN 1-58388-026-7
JUAN MANUEL FANGIO WORLD CHAMPION DRIVER SERIES PHOTO ALBUM	ISBN 1-58388-008-9
LE MANS 1950: PHOTO ARCHIVE THE BRIGGS CUNNINGHAM CAMPAIGN	ISBN 1-882256-21-2
MARIO ANDRETTI WORLD CHAMPION DRIVER SERIES PHOTO ALBUM	ISBN 1-58388-009-7
NOVI V-8 INDY CARS 1941-1965 LUDVIGSEN LIBRARY SERIES	ISBN 1-58388-037-2
SEBRING 12-HOUR RACE 1970 PHOTO ARCHIVE	ISBN 1-882256-20-4
VANDERBILT CUP RACE 1936 & 1937 PHOTO ARCHIVE	ISBN 1-882256-66-2

RAILWAYS

CHICAGO, ST. PAUL, MINNEAPOLIS & OMAHA RAILWAY 1880-1940 PHOTO ARCHIVE	ISBN 1-882256-67-0
CHICAGO & NORTH WESTERN RAILWAY 1975-1995 PHOTO ARCHIVE	ISBN 1-882256-76-X
GREAT NORTHERN RAILWAY 1945-1970 PHOTO ARCHIVE	ISBN 1-882256-56-5
GREAT NORTHERN RAILWAY 1945-1970 VOL 2 PHOTO ARCHIVE	ISBN 1-882256-79-4
MILWAUKEE ROAD 1850-1960 PHOTO ARCHIVE	ISBN 1-882256-61-1
MILWAUKEE ROAD DEPOTS 1856-1954 PHOTO ARCHIVE	ISBN 1-58388-040-2
SHOW TRAINS OF THE 20TH CENTURY	ISBN 1-58388-030-5
SOO LINE 1975-1992 PHOTO ARCHIVE	ISBN 1-882256-68-9
TRAINS OF THE TWIN PORTS, DULUTH-SUPERIOR IN THE 1950s PHOTO ARCHIVE	ISBN 1-58388-003-8
TRAINS OF THE CIRCUS 1872-1956	ISBN 1-58388-024-0
TRAINS of the UPPER MIDWEST PHOTO ARCHIVE STEAM&DIESEL in the1950S&1960S	ISBN 1-58388-036-4
WISCONSIN CENTRAL LIMITED 1987-1996 PHOTO ARCHIVE	ISBN 1-882256-75-1
WISCONSIN CENTRAL RAILWAY 1871-1909 PHOTO ARCHIVE	ISBN 1-882256-78-6

TRUCKS

BEVERAGE TRUCKS 1910-1975 PHOTO ARCHIVE	ISBN 1-882256-60-3
*BROCKWAY TRUCKS 1948-1961 PHOTO ARCHIVE**	ISBN 1-882256-55-7
CHEVROLET EL CAMINO PHOTO HISTORY INCL GMC SPRINT & CABALLERO	ISBN 1-58388-044-5
CIRCUS AND CARNIVAL TRUCKS 1923-2000 PHOTO ARCHIVE	ISBN 1-58388-048-8
DODGE PICKUPS 1939-1978 PHOTO ALBUM	ISBN 1-882256-82-4
DODGE POWER WAGONS 1940-1980 PHOTO ARCHIVE	ISBN 1-882256-89-1
DODGE POWER WAGON PHOTO HISTORY	ISBN 1-58388-019-4
DODGE RAM TRUCKS 1994-2001 PHOTO HISTORY	ISBN 1-58388-051-8
DODGE TRUCKS 1929-1947 PHOTO ARCHIVE	ISBN 1-882256-36-0
DODGE TRUCKS 1948-1960 PHOTO ARCHIVE	ISBN 1-882256-37-9
FORD HEAVY-DUTY TRUCKS 1948-1998 PHOTO HISTORY	ISBN 1-58388-043-7
JEEP 1941-2000 PHOTO ARCHIVE	ISBN 1-58388-021-6
JEEP PROTOTYPES & CONCEPT VEHICLES PHOTO ARCHIVE	ISBN 1-58388-033-X
LOGGING TRUCKS 1915-1970 PHOTO ARCHIVE	ISBN 1-882256-59-X
*MACK MODEL AB PHOTO ARCHIVE**	ISBN 1-882256-18-2
*MACK AP SUPER-DUTY TRUCKS 1926-1938 PHOTO ARCHIVE**	ISBN 1-882256-54-9
*MACK MODEL B 1953-1966 VOL 1 PHOTO ARCHIVE**	ISBN 1-882256-19-0
*MACK MODEL B 1953-1966 VOL 2 PHOTO ARCHIVE**	ISBN 1-882256-34-4
*MACK EB-EC-ED-EE-EF-EG-DE 1936-1951 PHOTO ARCHIVE**	ISBN 1-882256-29-8
*MACK EH-EJ-EM-EQ-ER-ES 1936-1950 PHOTO ARCHIVE**	ISBN 1-882256-39-5
*MACK FC-FCSW-NW 1936-1947 PHOTO ARCHIVE**	ISBN 1-882256-28-X
*MACK FG-FH-FJ-FK-FN-FP-FT-FW 1937-1950 PHOTO ARCHIVE**	ISBN 1-882256-35-2
*MACK LF-LH-LJ-LM-LT 1940-1956 PHOTO ARCHIVE**	ISBN 1-882256-38-7
*MACK TRUCKS PHOTO GALLERY**	ISBN 1-882256-88-3
NEW CAR CARRIERS 1910-1998 PHOTO ALBUM	ISBN 1-882256-98-0
PLYMOUTH COMMERCIAL VEHICLES PHOTO ARCHIVE	ISBN 1-58388-004-6
REFUSE TRUCKS PHOTO ARCHIVE	ISBN 1-58388-042-9
STUDEBAKER TRUCKS 1927-1940 PHOTO ARCHIVE	ISBN 1-882256-40-9
STUDEBAKER TRUCKS 1941-1964 PHOTO ARCHIVE	ISBN 1-882256-41-7
WHITE TRUCKS 1900-1937 PHOTO ARCHIVE	ISBN 1-882256-80-8

TRACTORS & CONSTRUCTION EQUIPMENT

CASE TRACTORS 1912-1959 PHOTO ARCHIVE	ISBN 1-882256-32-8
CATERPILLAR PHOTO GALLERY	ISBN 1-882256-70-0
CATERPILLAR POCKET GUIDE THE TRACK-TYPE TRACTORS 1925-1957	ISBN 1-58388-022-4
CATERPILLAR D-2 & R-2 PHOTO ARCHIVE	ISBN 1-882256-99-9
CATERPILLAR D-8 1933-1974 PHOTO ARCHIVE INCLUDING DIESEL 75 & RD-8	ISBN 1-882256-96-4
CATERPILLAR MILITARY TRACTORS VOLUME 1 PHOTO ARCHIVE	ISBN 1-882256-16-6
CATERPILLAR MILITARY TRACTORS VOLUME 2 PHOTO ARCHIVE	ISBN 1-882256-17-4
CATERPILLAR SIXTY PHOTO ARCHIVE	ISBN 1-882256-05-0
CATERPILLAR TEN PHOTO ARCHIVE INCLUDING 7C FIFTEEN & HIGH FIFTEEN	ISBN 1-58388-011-9
CATERPILLAR THIRTY PHOTO ARCHIVE 2ND ED. INC. BEST THIRTY, 6G THIRTY & R-4	ISBN 1-58388-006-2
CLETRAC AND OLIVER CRAWLERS PHOTO ARCHIVE	ISBN 1-882256-43-3
CLASSIC AMERICAN STEAMROLLERS 1871-1935 PHOTO ARCHIVE	ISBN 1-58388-038-0
FARMALL CUB PHOTO ARCHIVE	ISBN 1-882256-71-9
FARMALL F- SERIES PHOTO ARCHIVE	ISBN 1-882256-02-6
FARMALL MODEL H PHOTO ARCHIVE	ISBN 1-882256-03-4
FARMALL MODEL M PHOTO ARCHIVE	ISBN 1-882256-15-8
FARMALL REGULAR PHOTO ARCHIVE	ISBN 1-882256-14-X
FARMALL SUPER SERIES PHOTO ARCHIVE	ISBN 1-882256-49-2
FORDSON 1917-1928 PHOTO ARCHIVE	ISBN 1-882256-33-6
HART-PARR PHOTO ARCHIVE	ISBN 1-882256-08-5
HOLT TRACTORS PHOTO ARCHIVE	ISBN 1-882256-10-7
INTERNATIONAL TRACTRACTOR PHOTO ARCHIVE	ISBN 1-882256-48-4
INTERNATIONAL TD CRAWLERS 1933-1962 PHOTO ARCHIVE	ISBN 1-882256-72-7
JOHN DEERE MODEL A PHOTO ARCHIVE	ISBN 1-882256-12-3
JOHN DEERE MODEL B PHOTO ARCHIVE	ISBN 1-882256-01-8
JOHN DEERE MODEL D PHOTO ARCHIVE	ISBN 1-882256-00-X
JOHN DEERE 30 SERIES PHOTO ARCHIVE	ISBN 1-882256-13-1
MINNEAPOLIS-MOLINE U-SERIES PHOTO ARCHIVE	ISBN 1-882256-07-7
OLIVER TRACTORS PHOTO ARCHIVE	ISBN 1-882256-09-3
RUSSELL GRADERS PHOTO ARCHIVE	ISBN 1-882256-11-5
TWIN CITY TRACTOR PHOTO ARCHIVE	ISBN 1-882256-06-9

*This product is sold under license from Mack Trucks, Inc. Mack is a registered Trademark of Mack Trucks, Inc. All rights reserved.

All Iconografix books are available from direct mail specialty book dealers and bookstores worldwide, or can be ordered from the publisher. For book trade and distribution information or to add your name to our mailing list and receive a **FREE CATALOG** contact:

Iconografix, PO Box 446, Hudson, Wisconsin, 54016 Telephone: (715) 381-9755, (800) 289-3504 (USA), Fax: (715) 381-9756

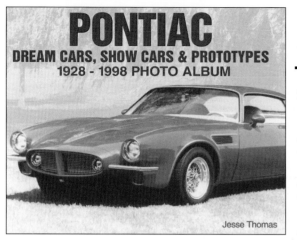
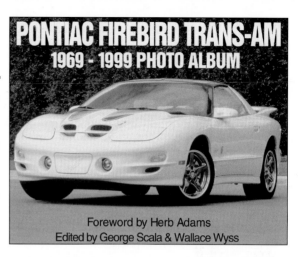
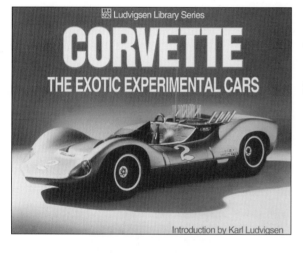
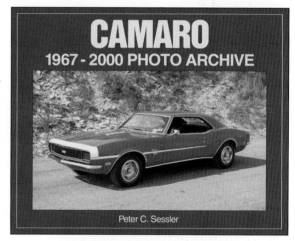
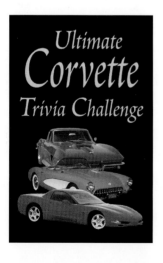
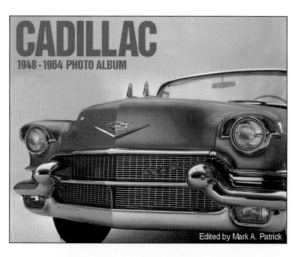
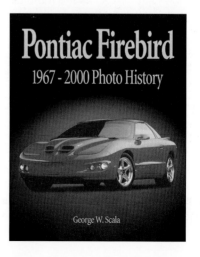

⊞ LUDVIGSEN LIBRARY LIMITED

The photographs in this book, supplied by the Ludvigsen Library, are available for purchase by enthusiasts. Based in London, this extensive automotive library, founded and owned by Karl Ludvigsen, is one of the world's most comprehensive sources of reference material about cars and the motor industry. Specializing in car and motor racing photography, it includes much rare and unpublished original material from John Dugdale, Edward Eves, Max Le Grand, Peter Keen, Karl Ludvigsen, Rodolfo Mailander, Ove Nielsen, Stanley Rosenthall and others.

All black and white prints are hand finished to museum display standards using the finest Ilford 1K fibre which gives a beautiful, durable finish that is perfect for mounting and display. Prints can be ordered from the Ludvigsen Library at the address below in three sizes at the following prices:

10 x 12	inches	US$40.00	UK£25.00
12 x 16	inches	US$55.00	UK£35.00
16 x 20	inches	US$75.00	UK£45.00

Please inquire concerning color, other sizes, and other subjects. Prices do not include packing and shipping fees, which will be advised in advance.

THE LUDVIGSEN LIBRARY LIMITED: 73 COLLIER STREET, LONDON N1 9BE, UNITED KINGDOM
TELEPHONE +44 (020) 7837 1700 FACSIMILE +44 (020) 7837 1776
E-MAIL LIBRARY@LUDVIGSEN.COM   HTTP://WWW.LUDVIGSEN.COM